THE WAY THINGS OUGHT TO BE:
REALLY!

By

Jim Green

DEDICATED TO:

FIX UNEMPLOYMENT, AND THIS WILL FIX THE MARKET: A 21st Century Solution—there is no more important mind-set in our 21st Century market economy – both economically and socially

ISBN-10: 198437866X

ISBN-13: 978-1984378668

PROLOGUE

Many of the things we do, today, are just plain stupid....which is "no no" language in good writing...but we do things that are inefficient—don't work— and in some cases are downright destructive to our civil order--and we seem to lack logic in looking for solutions,—or are just incapable of doing things differently...so we cling to the status quo.

As a result, I find myself using lots of exclamation marks in my frustration. Let me give an example:

I would like to write this like I was writing to President Obama, today—post presidency—and in the hopes that he is actually reading it....

President Obama:

Most of your presidency was a real credit to America—and anyone with an IQ above 3 knows that Trump is a racist idiot—which sums up the ignorance of his comments about your presidency!

But there is one area where you and the Democrats made a huge blunder—a blunder that was not only a loss to the American people—but put a cloud over your administration that you were never really able to shake…and cost you dearly, politically!

Specifically, you had a golden opportunity to fix unemployment [hereafter UE]—and you let the opportunity slip away--didn't fix it! When the Democrats held majorities in Congress and the White House—and full support of the America people—the honeymoon—the first 6 months, give or take, you had the opportunity to fully implement Pro-Market Humphrey-Hawkins—[hereafter HH--15 USC § 3101]--the most important legislation passed in the 20th Century—and it would have ended our unemployment crisis! Indeed, when I saw you going down the antiquated and unworkable "fix the market, and that will fix UE"—rather than the other way around—I thought "Oh no"—the Democrats don't get it—and as expected the 2010 election caught up with the error and filled the House with lunatics—which hounded you the rest of your presidency….

In fact, HH becomes more and more important with each passing year in our 21st Century market economy—with the proliferation of robots, alone!

And just from a political point of view you would have won Congress hands down in 2010—rather than lost in a disaster that followed you for the rest of your years in the WH....Further, your Job Creation was based on the absurd Republican scam [the Trump tax cut for the wealthy]on the premise that this will create jobs—IT IS PURE BS, and is the reason why it took you almost 8 years to shave even a miserable 5 points off of the UE rate! Further fixing unemployment never works with "jump start" funding--until the market kicks in—and will only work with "renewable funding"....Re: FIX UNEMPLOYMENT, AND THIS WILL FIX THE MARKET: A 21st Century Solution, Amazon

My guess is that many Democrats did not understand this law—and some never heard of it---and certainly didn't understand of its importance [unlike Congressman Conyers]—i.e., for all of the above reasons---and via a Social Insurance program we could have funded without adding a dime to our deficit!

My guess for you is that you just got bad advice—for one, Summers just didn't get it—in a few words—had HH been enacted, from 2009 on-- UE in America would have been restricted to 3%, PERMANENTLY!

The real reason we are stuck in the status quo, however, is one we don't discuss much---i.e., since WW II the Koch brothers [a metaphor, and fact, for the 1%-

-and with one foot still on the plantation] have spent hundreds of millions buying governors, legislators, Congress, etc., to abolish to the greatest extent possible "Employee Rights", in America—and to destroy our labor unions! Re: A POOL OF SLAVES TO BE USED AND DISCARDED "At Will"--Amazon

For instance, every state now has "at will" employment laws to deny Employee Rights [only Montana limits to probationary employees]—in short, our "Oligarchy"-- the 1% tell our politicians—"We bought and paid for your office—this is our province, so look the other way"—and only a few politicians are concerned that the American employee "has rights".....

Without implementation of HH, however, we limped along—prolonging the "misery index"--slowly eroding our 10% UE in 2009, to an anemic 5% --8 years later—and in the process fanning the flames, and with their growing resentment in Flint/the Rust Belt--ushering in the greatest mistake/disaster in America history: Thump's election!

The history of how HH came into existence, helps to understand its importance in our evolving economically and socially:

Since WW II, and living in the fear of McCarthyism— [our fear of being labeled a "commie"—and cowing under that fear]--our Job Creation in America [and to this day] has been framed around the fraudulent belief that "The market can provide anybody wanting a job, with a job"....it is PURE BS, and this model/policy for

Job Creation has not resulted in a UE rate below 3% since 1953! Leaving millions jobless in its wake, it has resulted in our inner-cities becoming war zones, with an epidemic of gun violence!

The mind-shattering question is: When this antiquated method of Job Creation obviously—DOESN'T WORK— [and with the past 8 years, alone, as consummate proof]---why do we keep doing it?

And, this milieu of miserable Job Creation, evident even by 1963, provided the impetus for the March on Washington in 1963, and the "I had a dream speech"— for JOBS! Consummate proof, even then [55 years ago!], that our method of Job Creation in America— DOESN'T WORK!

And every year thereafter civil rights leaders [including Jesse Jackson] marched on Dr. King's birthday—as the means to petition Congress to pass a JOBS bill!

As it turned out during a prolonged sluggish economy in 1978—the civil right leaders were finally successful in getting Congress to pass HH, which was then signed into law by President Carter.

Specifically, HH provides Congress with the "legal authorization" to create a "reservoir of public employees" anytime our UE rate rises above "3%"— and as noted, above, using a Social Insurance model we can implement without adding a dime to our deficit! See: THE NEIGHBOR-TO-NEIGHBOR JOB CREATION ACT [NTN--Amazon].

NTN is a deficit-neutral, pro-market, federally mandated Social Insurance, owned by our employed, to provide a fund to hire/train our unemployed. If one works in America, from the POTUS down, they would be automatically enrolled—with NTN triggered anytime our UE rate rises above 3%, per HH. Jobs beget jobs, and for a modest 4% of salary policy cost, and funded via FICA, we will create more "private-sector" jobs [our gold standard] in 6 months, per NTN, that our current method, HR 2847—in 6 years!

And, this is where bone-crushing frustration comes in….with a capital "S"—instead of implementing HH, the Democrat controlled Congress under Carter, stood on one foot and then the other and let Flint/the Rust Belt rot into decay…and as noted above—providing the seminal point for the political anger in that region—which ushered in Trump! Further, had Carter utilized a law he signed, to address our sluggish economy, then, via fixing UE—he would have won re-election hands down in 1980!

In short, the Democrats passed the most important law in the 20th Century—and then turned their back on the law--forgot it existed—i.e., were so blinded by the fraudulent belief that the market can provide all the jobs we need—they never implemented this landmark legislation—and it appears the Democrats/Obama administration suffered from the same malady—still clinging to the unworkable mind-set of the past…..

And as just one example of how myopic this view is: Research shows that 38% of American jobs will be lost to robots by 2030—so will our "leaders" still be standing on one foot, and then the other waiting on the market—in the face of a 38% UE rate? At what point will they wake up and accept that our status quo—DOESN'T WORK?

Another aspect of UE—which is never talked about—albeit is common sense---when even one employed person is no longer in the market, their income is lost to the economy—and while on an individual basis this is miniscule—when we throw in the almost 7 million the DOL "officially" report are looking for work, and can't find any [and by their own estimates the true number is closer to 15 million—the DOL does not count those who have stopped looking!]—*the loss of income to our economy has a substantial impact!*

So where is our economic index, like GDP—to warn us that: FULL EMPLOYMENT IS A PRO-MARKET SOLUTION, Amazon. Just saying that we have our UE rate--is insufficient—because it does not act as a warning light to the loss of income to the market as a result of UE…the bottom line is not factored in to signal the importance of employment—so we are still stuck in a plantation mind-set!

The fact is, UE is a NO ONE WINS: The jobless lose, civility loses [Ferguson, etc.,], and the market loses, to wit:

THE LAW OF DIMINISHED INCOME TO THE MARKET FROM UNEMPLOYMENT [hereafter D/UE LAW]

Short Definition:

3% is the zero-sum threshold above which unemployment starts substantially undermining the Market--and the loss in income to the Market is compounded exponentially with each percentage point of increase in unemployment, above 3%.

Internationally recognized economist, Dr. William Mitchell, has proposed a model, in concept like HH, which addresses our method of Job Creation in the 21st Century—as our jobs disappear to robots.....specifically: THE BUFFER STOCK EMPLOYMENT MODEL:

An expanding and contracting public work force that expands during downturns in the market, and contracts as employees return to the private sector. Ideally, this would be combined with HH—i.e., at any time our UE rate rises above 3%--this model would kick in to keep our UE rate at 3%--PERMANENTLY. It is an EVERYONE WINS, proposition....

Finally, the mind-set for public employment is that it is Pro-Market, and the truism that we have far more work that needs to be done in America, than we have persons to fill these jobs—the current notion that we need "make-work" jobs—is an absurd notion!

Another pet peeve [to put it in a civil tone] is how at risk our democracy has become since we have moved to electronic voting. Some parts are totally bizarre—with the corporations building the voting machines claiming ownership of the software which counts our votes—and the absence of a paper trail to verify election results!

And with the criminal CITIZEN UNITED allowing America to be put up for sale to the highest bidder—our "democracy" is now at extreme risk!

If Wal-Mart handed us a piece of paper with the words "trust us" as a receipt for our purchases—we wouldn't stand for it for a minute—and yet, this is a perfect metaphor for our current electronic voting system, in America—for instance, from the last election, alone, we know we have 3 million more Democrats than Republicans—and yet the Republicans and their GREED-DRIVEN agenda are running the show.....?

To respond to our pernicious electronic voting system, I created:

FAIL-SAFE ELECTRONIC VOTING

TO THE READER: Given you have gotten this far, and agree with the proposed changes—and particularly getting rid of the pernicious Citizens United—our democracy, and the above, or any, progress, will be in peril absent a "fail-safe" electronic voting system.

THE FAIL-SAFE ELECTRONIC VOTING ACT

1) EVERY electronic voting machine (hereafter EVM), must be inexpensive, identical throughout the U.S. in a 1/150 voter ratio, and *must count and produce a hard-copy of the recorded votes*. In addition, an extra copy of their recorded votes would be produced (not necessarily a hard-copy), marked "Voter's Copy", and containing "NOTICE: Do Not Destroy Until Every Election On Your Ballot Is Certified". [as noted: If Wal-Mart handed us a piece of paper with the words "trust us" as a receipt for our purchases—we would be outraged—and yet, this is our current electronic voting nightmare—but in this case it is our democracy at risk]!

2) *After confirming that their votes are recorded correctly*, the voter would then insert the hard-copy ballot into a software-free (count only) optical scanner (hereafter OS), for a second count. The hard-copy ballot would be retained by election officials in the event a candidate asks for a recount (*not possible under the current system, and which undermines the legality of each such election)*. The EVM and the OS must be manufactured by different companies (which is universally true today).

3) Election officials assigned to oversee the EVM, would be prevented by law from overseeing the OS, and vice-versa, and stiff criminal penalties would be imposed for violations.

4) Further, every EVM would be programmed with raw data re the total registration rolls, by party, and norms for their voting history, etc.,----as an "alert" to a

possible irregularity, such as an "under-vote"—or "vote-flipping" etc., and *standards* established to suspend certification where there is an "improbable result", at least temporarily, of a particular election until the discrepancy is cleared up. (This is what computers do best, and it would be very easy to create such a program).

5) At the end of the election day, tallies would be taken from the EVM and the OS, for each candidate. *If the tallies didn't balance for any given election, or if there is an "alert", that election cannot be certified until the "error" is corrected.* If the candidates agree (the victory is certain), minor discrepancies in the count could be disregarded. While probably rare, the Voter, or a random sample of Voters, would be required by law to return their Copy of the recorded votes to the election office to clear up any "error", or where an "alert" signals the need for same.

6) Further, every state provides for a recount when the total vote falls below a certain percent of difference between the candidates, impossible to conduct with the current EVM. And thus Congress must mandate the following regarding presidential candidates: A RUN-OFF election is mandated and triggered in those states where the percent of difference in the total vote is less than .5% between the two candidates; said election to be held on the second Saturday following the election, on PAPER BALLOTS ONLY, and contain ONLY the names of the relevant candidates, for instance: "Barack Obama, Democrat" and "John McCain, Republican"—with oversight in counting by a representative(s) of

each party—said procedure providing more than adequate time to meet the Electoral College mandate [Ideally, all of this could be eliminated if we did away with the Electoral College, but until then....]. NOTE: Had this been the law in 2000, Al Gore would be our president, and America would have been spared the economic, etc., disaster that followed!

7) Finally, absent the above safeguards, and until these safeguards are in place--Congress must mandate that PAPER BALLOTS, ONLY, can be used in our presidential elections. This is not a "partisan" issue, it is a "pro-democracy" issue. Most importantly, this will return the responsibility for our elections, and our vote counting, back into the hands of the individual voter, where it belongs, and out of the hands of "corporate control"---*it is* *after all "our democracy", itself, that is at risk if we don't take these steps---and in that regard, is there any time or cost differential that is too great?*

 Jim Green

Another concern—so transparent--it is a mind-shattering enigma why it is not in the national dialogue—let me explain it in this way:

Linking being a "Christian" and "voting Republican" in a sentence, or by any other means--is the most bizarre notion in America, today! The GREED-DRIVEN Republican agenda, today, is against EVERYTHING Christ stood for, and spoke out against! And yet, we have millions of Americans— mostly evangelicals—who march to the polls on election day and vote against the welfare of their own childrenm, by voting Republican!

By definition, a Christian is a person who is striving to follow Christ's teachings—why else would one call themselves a Christian? In short, voting Republican is an attack on Christianity—why on earth would anyone who calls themselves a Christian, do that? And their seeking a justification for voting Republican IS IMPOSSIBLE, because there is none!

We are, of course, all free to vote for any person, or party, we wish –and if someone wishes to vote against the welfare of their own children by voting Republican—i.e., a party that is looking out for the welfare of the Koch brothers—not them or their children—we can scratch our head at their incredible ignorance—and they can vote against Christianity—but they can't do both WITHOUT LYING TO THEMSELVES! They can't atate that they are following the tenents of Christianity, and vote Republican—WITHOUT LYING! Thus: IT IS IMPOSSIBLE TO BE A CHRISTIAN, AND VOTE REPUBLICAN [Amazon]—PERIOD

Finally, this faction is the reason Washington is in total chaos! We can't have a significant segment of the members of Congress, who are there based on this incredible ignorance—i.e. persons who so ill-informed of the GREED-DRIVEN agenda of the Republican agenda—they vote against everything Christ stood for, and spoke our against—and in their bubble, actually think they are Christians!

Another pet peeve—a "why on earth are we doing this?"—is the war of words we have between what we call "socialism", and "capitalism"—it is like we are still cowing—like a bunch cowards—from the wrost terrorist in American history—McCarthyism! Capitalism would fold in a NY second were it not for the two trillion in taxes being infused back into our economy by Washington [socialism--BOO]—and were it not for the $800 billion from Social Security [socialism—BOO] percolating up through our economy in 2009—WE WOULD BE BURIED IN ANOTHER GREAT DEPRESSION!

The truth is, capitalism is ideal in producing and selling corn flakes and cars—It is miserable at solving "social problems" such as unemployment and our healthcare....

And when we have tried "privatization" to solve our social problems—it has been a disaster:

Specifically, essential programs have been cut—such as the elimination of text books from the Job Corps education program—to increase profits, and cronyism has run rampant—

And in our "for profit" healthcare system, billions of dollars are siphoned away from the premiums we send in—and do not go to the healthcare of ANYONE—but rather is used to pay for lobbyists, to make the CEO's filthy rich—and spent on propaganda ads to keep it that way!

Further, it attracts a few who see healthcare as a means to get rich, rather than cure the ill....

The truth is, we currently have a blended economic system—and they are, in fact, both interdependent to, and indispensable to each other:

Social Insurance is a vital ingredient in building a vibrant and decent society—And, invent a better widget, sell the company for a million bucks, and retire in Florida [capitalism]—is as well a vital ingredient in building a vibrant and decent society. [I am a capitalist—support capitalism 1000%--always have been, always will be]!

So why do we have this war of words pitting the two against each other—rather than educating the American people regarding the indispensable symbiotic relationship they have to each other?

And yet, most Republicans ask God in their prayers at night to be protected from communists, or socialists, or even worse "liberals"—[i.e., monsters under their bed] with "liberal" henceforth to be replaced witht the word "Christian".....

And this war of words disguises that the Republican Party, today, is not the Pro-Market party they boast—but rather their policies are, in fact, Anti-Market—destructive to capitalism!

Pandering to the GREED of their wealthiest contributors—the Republican One and Only program, today—is NOT Pro-Market—it is destructive to a market economy, for the reasons cited!

Regarding "unemployment" —it is essential that we evolve, and given "automation/robots", alone, in our 21st Century economy we need to look upon UE the same as we look upon Cancer, Polio, or AIDS, as a ubiquious disease—a menace to society, in need of eradication....using "public employment" to keep UE low is a PRO-MARKET concept—and it is only those who are basking in ignorance—who don't understand this!

And, 95% of our social ills—including Prison Reform-- would be addressed, over night, if we enforced the "legal authorization" we already have on the books in America [15 USC § 3101]—and restrict our UE rate in America to 3%, permanently!

My next pet peeve—is mind-shattering in many respects—why we allow the Republican party—IN THE NAME OF PURE GREED—to rob the American people blind with their Supply-Side scam—FOR THE

THIRD TIME SINCE 1980! See: SUPPLY-SIDE REFRIED, Amazon

From Reagan on, their scam speech has always been the same—from Reagan, thru Bush, and now Trump--- "The ultra-wealthy are paying way too much in taxes" [such rot!]…..and if we cut those taxes the market will blossom, and jobs will rain down like moon-beams—IT IS PER BS!

And in the first year of each of their administrations they have given massive tax cuts to the wealthy [and always with the blatant lie that it is "tax reform"]! And then they started driving up the deficit so that the cost of this "gift to the wealthy" is passed on to the American people, and our children and grandchildren! Never, in the scripture did Christ say "steal from the poor to give to the rich" Another reason why it is impossible to be a Christian, and vote Republican!

But about jobs raining down like moonbeams—as we learned in 1987 and 2008—this criminal scam has a self-life max of 7 years—before the economy goes into meltdown—and in the process millions of jobs are lost—trillions are added to the taxes of the American people, and trillions added to our deficit to buy our way out of this criminal scam—and prevent another Great Depression! In truth, it should be a "LOCK THEM UP" scam pulled on the American people, by the Republicans!

Specifically, on October 19, 1987—the Stock Market lost a quarter of its value on that day—the largest one day decline since the Great Depression;

And, the Stock Market crash in the Fall of 2008--on September 29, 2008—with a 777 point loss on that day--the loss of 700,000 jobs a month, for months—and resulting in a staggering 10% UE rate for most of the next year!

And how the Republicans can keep a straight face—and tell their BALD-FACE LIES about Supply-Side to the American people—escapes me—calling them "psychopaths" just isn't a big enough word!

Also, with rare exception….show me a Republican in Congress, today, and I'll show you an INSUFFERABLE JERK—[to the person they voted for Trump's tax cut for the wealthy]---Like Cotton from Arkansas….what a CREEP…..and bottom-feeder…like Trump, pandering to his racist faction and scum who want to relegate America to the 8th Century, BC---and what does this tell us about the folk who voted to put them there…who inexplicably call themselves "Christians"?

Further, from Reagan on the Koch brothers [a metaphor, and fact for the 1%]—stuffed the windfall of cash from their tax cut, in their pocket, or built factories in Sri Lanka, and fraudulently hid their profits in the Cayman Islands—to defraud investing in America! And since Reagan on, this Republican scam has resulted the greatest wealth disparity in American history!

Another pet peeve is our myopia in not recognizing that work must be come a "legal right"—we'll get there---it is central to social/economic evolution—but for now we still languish on the plantation—by the small-minded who want employees to show up with hat in hand—and expect to get their butt kissed for the job....but these jerks are dying out, and of very late we have had a mass of sexual harassment charges raised by women—part and parcel of the same dying mind-set....

The right to work and be a productive member of society was a given in primitive societies [indeed expected]—but lost in the Age of Industrialization—to the detriment of civilization! The right to be a productive member of society should be recognized as a human right—and 95% of our social-ills would disappear if it were recognized--but the "hat in hand" jerks are still here trying to make life as miserable as possible—their objective....but they are dying off......and if we don't blow ourselves up—they will disappear as we evolve.....

The next is more of an outrage, rather than a pet peeve—the fact that Democrats don't seem to catch on they are in A DOG FIGHT WITH A JUNKYARD DOG [Amazon]—with the Republicans! When the very recent sexual harassment flap started the Democrats demanded the "perpetrators" resign their positions in Congress [when we are already far from a majority]—but not the Republicans—take Trump, for example, he

just denied [in the face of over whelming evidence]—
and resign, not a chance [yet]—

Another example—among our legitimate journalists—
and legitimate news organizations [most of whom are
Democrats because we are on the right side of
history]—but if they are not right on the nose with the
truth—they get fired—as opposed to FAUX—where
lying gets them promoted for lying!-

The message to Democrats is: GET A SPINE! And
recognize the kind of fight you are in—and respond in
kind!

Another area that is an enigma, to me, because it seems
so obvious: Why do we cling to the archaic belief: FIX
THE MARKET, AND THIS WILL FIX
UNEMPLOYMENT----rather than the other way
around….the former is the reason the
Democrats/Obama were unable to fix UE—to the
detriment to EVERYONE! Indeed, HR 2847—their so
called JOBS bill was framed around fixing the market
on the premise that this would fix unemployment—but
like all "trickle down"—the jobs didn't come about fast
enough, or far enough—and evident by the result—a
crummy 5% in 8 years! In short, we need to get real:
FIX UNEMPLOYMENT, AND THIS WILL FIX THE
MARKET!

And like most of the above, it is OUR GREED AND
IGNORANCE [Amazon] that keeps us stuck in the 8th
Century—BC—when we let the Republicans in the
White House!

Finally, is not a negative—but a positive program I have come up with to address our problems as we go into the 21st Century: ECONOMIC INCLUSIVISM – NEO-CAPITALISM [Amazon/Kindle]:

Central to all else is bringing our Job Creation into the modern world—into our 21st Century market economy--articulated above—and foremost is the mind-set: Fix UE, and this will fix the market—rather than the other way around—i.e., Neo-capitalism is a Pro-Market concept--high unemployment/sluggish economy is not a non sequitur!

To get into specifics in problem solving via Economic Inclusivism:

THE THEORY OF ECONOMIC INCLUSIVISM:
A 21st Century Solution

[Social/Prison Reforms]

1) We need to re-classify all crime in the future as violent or non-violent, and discard the archaic terms felony and misdemeanor. The word felony has been implanted in the public's mind to mean "armed and dangerous", and yet over 70% of our prison inmates (all felons) are in prison for non-violent offenses. As a result, the term "felony" is distracting us from addressing the real problem....the violent offender.

2) We need a much greater use of "Shock"

Incarceration (A sentencing alternative I authored in the 1960's); a greater use of fines, restitution, and probation (both civil and criminal), in lieu of incarceration, and fines paid directly to victims instead of the state all as part of an expanded menu of sentencing alternatives. [We have 5% of the world's population, and 25% of all prison inmates on earth, in our prisons! If we had the same proportion of inmates to general population as the rest of the civilized world, we would have 400,000 persons incarcerated, not 2,200,000, as we do at present! And yet our PR is that we are the most free country in the world? We daily turn non-violent persons into violent career criminals, with over 99% released back into society, making life in America MORE dangerous, not less! And the grizzly stabbing death, in Illinois, of 8 and 9 year old girls, on Mother's Day, 2005, by a recently released inmate, is a textbook example of this inept approach..when on earth are we going to accept that to whatever degree....we are also part of the problem? Prison should be a last resort, not first!] We can correct this by mandating that our legislatures return to the pre-1988 (pre the Willie Horton ad) standard: For every $1 budgeted for prisons, $5 MUST be budgeted for the education of our children. This appx ratio was not set by statute, but rather by tradition and common sense. At present, we budget more for prisons than educating our youth, and were not becoming a police state?

3) We need to create Federal Regional Diagnostic and Treatment Centers, for the diagnosis and treatment of the violent offender. We have learned a great deal about violent behavior in recent years (see

www.brainplace.com), and yet we do not have a cohesive or concerted national program or policy in America for dealing with this national epidemic and disgrace. The sheer numbers of homicides by handguns, alone, tells the whole story: Canada 151, Australia 57, Germany 373, Japan 19, England and Wales 54, the United States 11,789! When we add in all deaths by guns, including the fact that 9 children are killed by guns everyday in America, our gun violence escalates to a staggering 28,663! Also, we need to allow for voluntary admissions to these Centers, to prevent juvenile and family violence. It is essential that we seek out "problem-solving", not "punishment" oriented solutions, which actually exacerbate crime.

4) We need to pick-up the lead taken by England, in treating drug addiction as a "medical" rather than a "criminal" problem, so that we can EFFECTIVELY curb drug-related crime, and keep drugs out of the hands of our youth. To demonstrate how specious our thinking has become in this area, alcohol and tobacco kill ten of thousands of persons annually, and yet these drugs are not classified as "dangerous". The tiny handful of persons with "addictive personalities" has totally shaped our drug policies while "addiction", in all of its forms, can only EFFECTIVELY be treated with a medical solution. We have wasted billions on interdiction, and yet, youth drug abuse is actually increasing.

[Economic Reforms]

5) To address our insidious practice of "exclusion",

Congress must enforce a citizen's legal right to work (1), as enacted by Congress in "The Full Employment Act of 1946", and as outlined in the Democratic National Platform position asserting "Opportunity to every American". The right to work and be a productive member of one's society is also a human right. Accordingly, we must ratify the following constitutional amendment: "Work shall hereafter be the legal right of every citizen, and Congress shall, except for retirement/disability programs under federal jurisdiction, make no laws which will abridge the right of any citizen of legal age, to work and be a productive citizen." [Our lapse in enlightenment regarding this urgently needed systemic change -- believed by the ignorant and uninformed to be "communism" -- combined with some really peculiar notions about guns, is the cause for almost all violent crime in America. This is a practical rather than a liberal solution in our 21st Century economy, a point totally lost on ideologues. This is not a safety net (the conservative propaganda buzz term to undermine social programs), this is recognizing within each of us as a human right. The distinction is as different as night and day. Further, rather than being a wildly radical idea, a recent Zogby poll found that "86% of Americans think the government should provide a job to anyone who wants one", according to the April 4, 2005 issue of The Nation. Economic Inclusivism, however, does not ask that the government provide a job, but rather recognizes within each citizen the legal right to work and be a productive member of the society, as a HUMAN RIGHT. We will always have government controls so that we have safe food, and medicine, etc., and we rightfully should have, that is separate and apart from the government doing, what a free enterprise business can do better. I would vehemently disagree that our recognition within each citizen a human right to work and be a productive citizen to be an interference with the free enterprise system, and full employment would have more of a psychological impact on the individual, than an economic impact on the economy, as it currently exists. A person wishing to become a doctor, will still become a doctor, or a CEO, or bartender, whatever....people do what is most compatible with their nature and talents and Economic Inclusivism would not change that. Indeed, in some cases it would provide a greater assist in their reaching their goal, than is currently available, and it is much more efficient in utilizing our greatest resource: humans, that our current system. Most importantly, it is the right thing to do!

6) To ensure enforcement/fund this legal right, Congress would create a privately owned, federally mandated, Social Insurance, with limited ownership by each person who works, which would provide work/training to any citizen who applies. Work could include: Child care for low income working families, building a high-speed rail system, the urgent need outlined by the NEA for School Modernization, the creation of Federal Regional Diagnostic and Treatment Centers for the diagnosis and treatment of the violent offender [HINT: convert our excessive new prisons into said Centers], repairing our rotting infrastructure (the list of social benefits is endless).

7) Since this program of "inclusion" would address 95% of our social ills (crime, welfare, drugs, etc., and exacerbated in many cases by inept Band-Aid programs), the federal budget could be greatly reduced and our current Federal Income Tax would be replaced with a National Sales Tax, value-added tax, a national lottery, or some combination of taxes other than our current Federal Income Tax. We currently spend 26 billion annually for the Internal Revenue Service, and corporations and individuals spend trillions trying to get around the Tax Code, all of which is passed on to us, the consumer, in the higher cost of consumer goods.

7a)A Universal Healtcare System is an essential ingredient of a sane society!

A few closing comments in the Prologue—As Oscar Wilde averred "The only truly worthless opinion is an unbiased one"—so bias, agreed—but always in the interest in getting at the larger goal—the truth....

Incidentally, I published my first book on my 78th birthday [I am currently 83]—and not that I write that fast, or well—the materials were all there for the better part of the past 30 years, give or take, gathering dust— it was just a matter of pulling them together in some order—also, don't believe any book should be over 60 pages, plus/minus— i.e., can be read in the crapper-- two hours, max--lol—but it seems best summed up by a very astute observer [wish I could recall their name to give credit]: Persons who write do so because they have no choice [it is a compulsion, an addiction..]—they become an "author", however, when people start reading what they have written...

Finally, a note to the reader—the papers and letters to expand on the above are not in sequence, and apologize for redundancy [please look for the nuggets...Thx--lol]—also, if you are a "typo-wonk"—are more concerned with sentence structure, etc., than content—you probably won't like my writing—and you will find a wayward capital letter, here and there, and appearing out of place and used for emphasis—or a missing page...Hey, I'm and Indie....I chalk most up to editorial license and tongue-in-cheek, self-effacing humor—so apologies, here—[I seriously support: Take what you do seriously, but never yourself....]....

Just look for content, please....THX

CHAPTER ONE

President Obama/Presidential Innovation Fellows:

Since WW II our single method of Job Creation in America has been based on the belief/propaganda that "The market can provide anybody wanting a job, with a job"......

And when it didn't work--we pretended it did, and drifted into Santa Clause-like wishful thinking— asserting "it is the American way", or "God's will"—or some such lie we told ourselves--as rational Job Creation, in a changing world, drifted further and further away.....

For instance, this method of Job Creation has not resulted in a UE rate below 3% since 1953, but we limped along—terrorized by McCarthyism, and leaving millions jobless—and by the mid-1970's the colliding forces of globalization, automation, technology reached critical mass, resulting in a cosmic shift in the world economy—with subsequent "High and persistent unemployment pervasive throughout the OECD since the mid-1970's", according to Dr. William F. Mitchell, and every credible economist.

And, going forward the data got even more grim—i.e., since 1980 we have had excessive UE 70% of the time [twice that of preceding years], and by the Crash of 2008—8 million were rendered jobless—[and in spite of an extremely anemic recovery we inched down from

10% to 5% UE, inexplicably still relying on the above method]——-

And with the result that by the September 2016 DOL Jobs Report, we still have 8 million Americans looking for work, that can't find any…..and in an economy limping along on a flat tire—as a direct result of high UE, and a Republican Congress determined to sabotage America—for political reasons--

The lesson is: Our choices are adapt and change in a world that is changing—whether we like it or not—or be forced to create a Police State to hold in place antiquated and unworkable laws and policies [in this case re our Job Creation]—and sadly, America has opted for the latter—and we need look no further than the police marching in lock-step in Charlotte, this past week, as proof!

The flaw in all of this is based on simple common sense: "The mechanic can't fix the engine without the proper tools"—and when Jobs, Jobs, Jobs is the major mantra in this election—fixing unemployment is hopeless so long as we insist on a method of Job Creation—THAT DOESN'T WORK!

Proposed Solutions: HR 1000, and FULL EMPLOYMENT IS A PRO-MARKET CONCEPT, Amazon

Jim Green, Democrat opponent to Lamar Smith, 2000

Thank you for contacting the White House!

CHAPTER TWO

President Obama/Council of Economic Advisers:

Capitalism is ideal in producing and selling corn flakes and cars—It doesn't work in solving "social problems" such as unemployment and our healthcare....

And when we have tried "privatization" to solve our social problems—it has been a disaster:

Specifically, essential programs have been cut—such as the elimination of text books from the Job Corps education program—to increase profits, and cronyism has run rampant—

And in our "for profit" healthcare system, billions of dollars are siphoned away from the premiums we send in—and do not go to the healthcare of ANYONE—but rather is used to pay for lobbyists, to make the CEO's filthy rich—and spent on propaganda ads to keep it that way!

Additionally, President Obama had a weapon in 2009, not available to FDR: Were it not for the $800 billion in Social Security Insurance moneys percolating up through our economy annually, ie., in 2008—we would

not be talking about having narrowly averted another Great Depression—We would be buried in one!

The truth is, we have a blended economic system—and the two components are, in fact, indispensable to each other:

Social Insurance is a vital ingredient in building a vibrant and decent society—And, invent a better widget, sell the company for a million bucks, and retire in Florida [capitalism]—is as well a vital ingredient in building a vibrant and decent society.

So why do we have this war of words pitting the two against each other—rather than educating the American people regarding the indispensable symbiotic relationship they have to each other?

Were it not for the $2 trillion + Washington infuses back into the economy annually—capitalism would fold in a NY Second!

And yet, most Republicans ask God in their prayers at night to be protected from communists, or socialists, or even worse "liberals"—[i.e., monsters under their bed] with "liberal" henceforth to be replaced with the word "Christian"…..

Regarding "unemployment" [hereafter UE]—it is essential that we evolve, and given "automation", alone, in our 21ˢᵗ Century economy we need to look upon UE the same as we look upon Cancer, Polio, or AIDS, as a ubiquious disease—a menace to society, in need of eradication….via [15 USC § 3101]—which would restrict our UE to 3%, permanently!

Re: IT IS IMPOSSIBLE TO BE A CHRISTIAN, AND VOTE REPUBLICAN, Amazon/Kindle

Jim Green, Democrat opponent to Lamar Smith, 2000

Thank you for contacting President Obama.

CHAPTER THREE

President Obama/Council of Economic Advisers:

Every credible economist agrees that "High and persistent unemployment has pervaded almost every OECD country since the mid-1970's"….and almost 1 in 2 Americans [43%] cite Job Creation as the Number One issue in the 2016 election….

And yet, addressing the devastating results of unemployment [hereafter UE], as a stand-alone problem, to be solved the same as we would look upon a pandemic, is not in any of the debates, and while all of our candidates say they will create JOBS, our current solution to UE is analogous to not putting gas in our car, and then puzzling over why it doesnl't run…..and we need look no further than Flint, to understand the devastating results of UE…..

For instance, since WW II, the American people have been sold a Bill of Goods that "the market can provide anybody wanting a job, with a job"—which the data shows to be pure BS….and only ONCE since WW II has this Job Creation methodology resulted in a UE rate below 3%--in 1953—leaving millions jobless in its wake—and resulting in our inner-cities becoming war zones, with an epidemic of gun violence…..

And while all of the candidates talk about how they will create jobs, the REAL issue--the adverse consequences of unemployment —both to the jobless and the market...never gets discussed.....i.e., UE is a NO ONE WINS...the jobless lose, civility loses [Ferguson, etc.], and the market loses, to wit:

THE LAW OF DIMINISHED INCOME TO THE MARKET FROM UNEMPLOYMENT [hereafter D/UE LAW]

> 3% is the zero-sum threshold above which unemployment triggers inflation by diminishing labor training and skills, under-utilizing capital resources, reducing the rate of productivity advance, increasing unit labor costs, reducing the general supply of goods and services--and the loss in income to the Market is compounded exponentially with each percentage point of increase in unemployment, above 3%.

Finally, it would be ideal if the market could provide all of the jobs we need—but pretending that the market can provide a solution it is INCAPABLE of providing is analogous to our putting a lawnmower engine in the Saturn V rocket to the Moon.....

Ref: HR 1000 [in Committee]; THE NEIGHBOR-TO-NEIGHBOR JOB CREATION ACT, and FULL EMPLOYMENT IS A PRO-MARKET CONCEPT, Amazon, Kindle

Jim Green, Democrat opponent to Lamar Smith, Congress, 2000

CC: Donald Trump

CHAPTER FOUR

To The Honorable President Obama:

HR 1000 [In Committee] IS INDISPENSABLE IN OUR WINNING THE WAR AGAINST TERRORISM

This letter is to urge you to award the Presidential Medal of Freedom to U.S. Representative John Conyers, from Michigan.

Not only is he the longest-serving member of Congress—he has tirelessly worked for the Full Employment of Americans [HR 1000, in Committee], and in addressing inequity in America—a Renaissance Man in our 21st Century economy, who was present in Selma, on Freedom Day, October 7, 1963.

Further, Representative Conyers has made "an especially meritorious contribution to the security or national interests of the United States, world peace, cultural or other significant public or private endeavors" [the purpose for this award].

Few Americans are more deserving.

Finally, his appointment will call attention to the most important legislation in the 20th Century in our War On Terrorism, and indispensable to the effective functioning of our 21st Century market economy—pro-market Humphrey-Hawkins Full Employment Act, signed into law by President Carter [15 USC § 3101]. We have had excessive unemployment 70% of the time since 1980 as a result of automation/globalization, alone, and the implementation of this law [integral to HR 1000] will address the number one issue in the 2016 election: Jobs in our 21st Century market economy.

Ref: FULL EMPLOYMENT IS A PRO-MARKET CONCEPT, Amazon/Kindle

With highest regards,

Jim Green, Democrat candidate for Congress, District 21, TX, 2000

Thank you for contacting the White House!

CHAPTER FIVE

President Obama/Council of Economic Advisers:

"The truth is poetry, problem is—most people hate poetry" Mark Twain

What if you knew something that would eradicate terrorism…but because of tradition, resistance to change, etc., your information is not readily understood….but at the risk of being stereotyped by the GE ad, and for the sake of discussion—here goes:

First, it needs to be understood that the most dangerous belief afoot in America today, is "the market can provide anybody wanting a job, with a job"—and while every Republican in Congress believes it to be true—it is dangerous, because it is PURE BS……

Indeed, so prevalent is this belief that it has dominated our Job Creation since WW II—and in spite of the fact that this has resulted in an unemployment [hereafter UE] rate below 3% only ONCE since WW II—in 1953—leaving millions jobless in its wake since, and has resulted in 60% minority UE in our inner-cities, drug economies, and an epidemic of gun violence —

Also, with the proliferation of automation, alone, in the mid-1970's, and subsequent loss of employment, we have had excessive UE 70% of the time in the U.S., since 1980—

Further, as a result of the paradigm shift in the 1970's, UE is accelerating the further we advance into the 21st Century....i.e., with 10% UE now common in the Eurozone--25% in Greece and Spain....and UE was a major factor in Arab Spring....

And here is where common sense comes in.....we need look no further than Flint, to understand the devastating results of UE, and statistics show that with each point of increase in the UE rate, 40,000 die in ancillary damage!

And yet, in spite of the damage, we have yet to identify UE as a "social" problem, ever bit as damaging as a pandemic—i.e., WE, as the larger society, have a solemn responsibility to address...but which we ignore with the rationalization that "No sweat, the market has this covered"....and Flint is the result.....

Finally, in this dynamic, the right to work and be a productive member of society was a given in primitive societies—but lost in the Age of Industrialization--and the indifference by the larger society to the importance of employment [inclusion], has become a breeding ground for terrorism.....

Ref: HR 1000 [in Committee], ECONOMIC INCLUSIVISM, and FULL EMPLOYENT IS A PRO-MARKET CONCEPT, Amazon/Kindle

Jim Green, Democrat opponent to Lamar Smith, 2000

Thank you for contacting the White House!

CHAPTER SIX

President Obama/Council of Economic Advisers:

Our current method of Job Creation in America is a miserable failure—our proof is the fact that the number one issue in the 2016 election is JOBS—and we have had excessively high unemployment [hereafter UE] 70% of the time since 1980—[double that in prior years] with automation, alone, accelerating our UE the further we advance into the 21st Century…..

In truth, the world has changed and our UE crisis, with 20 million jobless Americans, is mired in the 18th Century as a result of Job Creation policies which have one foot on the plantation---in a 21st Century market economy--

Since WW II the oligarchy has spent tens of millions [buying elections/politicians] to look the other way, and turn their back on the will of the American people—i.e., and let the oligarchy write our Job Creation policy in America—it is based on the propaganda/lie that "the market can provide anybody wanting a job, with a job"—which the data shows to be Pure BS—

That is, only ONCE since WW II has this method of Job Creation resulted in a UE rate below 3%--in 1953—leaving millions jobless in its wake, and has resulted in 60% minority UE in our inner-cities, drug economies, and an epidemic of gun violence!

We need look no further than Flint to understand the destructive effects of unemployment—and WE are a "can do" nation—but when it comes to our Job Creation in America, our policies could be compared to our scientists putting a lawnmower engine in the Saturn 5 Rocket to the Moon…..

And the over-arching question, today, is: When our method of job creation doesn't work….why on God's earth do we continue down this path? And, particularly given the pervasive damage caused by UE--This criticism is not anti-capitalism—it is a statement of fact!

And ignored in all of this is that "We have far more work that needs to be done in America, than we have persons to fill these jobs", and "86% of Americans believe that anybody wanting to work should be able to find a job"…..UE is a NO ONE WINS: The jobless lose, civility loses [Ferguson, etc.,]…..

And, the Market loses!

INDISPENSABLE to the EFFECTIVE functioning of our market economy going forward in the 21st Century is: HR 1000 [in

Committee], and/or THE NEIGHBOR-TO-
NEIGHBOR JOB CREATION ACT,
Amazon/Kindle—or like Job Creation....

Jim Green, Democrat opponent to Lamar
Smith, 2000

CHAPTER SEVEN

This is an election year, why is this being ignored by the media?

President Obama/Council of Economic Advisers:

We need look no further than Flint to understand the destructive effects of unemployment [hereafter UE]---- as destructive to a community as a pandemic—

And yet, we—as the larger society—are prepared to pool all of our resources to eradicate a pandemic with all deliberate speed—but we turned our back and run the other way from the destruction to Flint—i.e., we allowed Flint to fall into decay as a result of UE— indeed, we have a "Rust Belt" in America, because of the same phenomenon.

Problem is, Washington pretends all of this is normal— A position not shared by the tens of thousands that are showing up to protest at rallies--for Sanders and Trump....

Michael Moore has documented the destruction of Flint in "Roger and Me"—which went from a thriving community of 80,000, with little crime, in the 1970's— to 50,000 by 1990, with 60% minority UE, the highest violent crime rate in America, and an epidemic of gun violence....

And while the focus by Moore was on the "unjustified" plant closings by GM--it was a missed opportunity to focus on UE as a "social" problem we as the larger society have a fiduciary obligation to address......

After all, we should never condemn a CEO who closes a plant because they are losing money [which Moore asserts did not apply to GM]—but we are outraged by a government that is indifferent to finding a solution.

And the irony is that in 1978 [perfect timing to rescue Flint], President Carter signed into law a "legal authorization" to restrict our UE rate to "3%" permanently [15 USC § 3101]—i.e., at no time, and to this day, should the UE rate in Flint, or anywhere else in America, exceed 3%--so why, and to this day, does Washington pretend this law doesn't exist?

The answer underscores the criminality in Citizens United—and the hundreds of millions spent buying our elections since WW II, and the warning from the 1% to bought and paid for politicians: Noli Tangere [do not touch] Job Creation in America—the result has been a disaster, and only ONCE since WW II has 1% Job Creation resulted in a UE rate below 3%--in 1953---leaving millions jobless in its wake, and our inner-cities a mirror image of Flint!

Ref: HR 1000 [in Committee]; THE CASE FOR WORK BEING A LEGAL RIGHT, and FULL EMPLOYMENT IS A PRO-MRKET CONCEPT, Amazon/Kindle

Jim Green, Democrat opponent to Lamar Smith, 2000

Thank you for contacting the White House!

CHAPTER EIGHT

President Obama:

When you took office it appeared—finally, and with a Democrat house and senate—that we would finally fix unemployment [hereafter UE] in America.

And particularly since the mantra, and getting louder in every election since 1980, has been FIX UNEMPLOYMENT. In fact, we have had excessive UE 70% of the time since 1980 [double that of preceding years].

According to Dr. William F. Mitchell, and every credible economist, "High and persistent unemployment has pervaded almost every OECD country since the mid-1970's".

And in 1978, the U.S. took a proactive step by providing a "legal authorization" to end our unemployment crisis [15 USC § 3101], and least understood is that implementation of this law is Pro-Market—i.e., given automation, alone, our taking this step is INDISPENSABLE to the EFFECTIVE functioning of our 21st Century market economy.

Since WW II the archaic model we have been operating under [and bought and paid for in our elections by the plutocracy/oligarchy] is "fix the market, and this will fix unemployment", rather than "fix unemployment and this will fix the market"—

And running in parallel is the most pernicious propaganda in America, today, i.e., that "the market can provide anybody wanting a job, with a job"—it is pure BS—and only ONCE since WW II has this Job Creation model resulted in a UE rate below 3%--in 1953—leaving millions jobless in its wake, and leaving our inner-cities with 60% minority UE, drug economies, and an epidemic of gun violence!

In any event, when we Democrats failed to fix UE, a retaliatory electorate filled the House with lunatics in the 2010 election, and DC has been in paralysis ever since......and also accounts for the masses showing up at Sanders/Trump rallies....

For clarity of the above...Humphrey-Hawkins is brilliant, ahead of its time—more valuable with each passing year—and incredibly misunderstood.......i.e., had Carter enforced the "legal authorization" in this law, he signed--and, in fact, reduced our UE rate to "3%" as provided for in the law—there is no way he would have lost the election to Reagan.......

Deficit-Neutral Solutions: HR 1000 [in Committee]; THE NEIGHBOR-TO-NEIGHBOR JOB CREATION ACT, and THE CASE FOR WORK BEING A LEGAL RIGHT, Amazon/Kindle

Jim Green, Democrat opponent to Lamar Smith, 2000 Bio: http://www.amazon.com/James-L.-Jim-Green/e/B001KHZIMM/ref=ntt_dp_epwbk_0

Thank you for contacting the White House!

CHAPTER NINE

President Obama/Council of Economic Advisers:

We do not currently have a legal right to work because we are living in the dark ages—in denial re automation, alone, in our 21st Century market economy--to the detriment of the market!

In fact, we have had excessive unemployment [hereafter UE] 70% of the time since 1980 [twice that of preceding years] as the result of a paradigm shift, an adjustment towards modernity, in the world economy in the mid-1970's—resulting from the colliding forces of globalization, automation, technology, etc., reaching critical mass.

Indeed, the U.S. responded directly to this paradigm shift with Pro-Market landmark legislation in 1978 [15 USC § 3101], to lawfully limit our UE rate in America to 3% permanently, henceforth—but in a desperate effort to cling to the past and maintain the status quo, the Koch brothers [a metaphor, here, for the 1%] bought off Washington via our elections—to prevent this law from ever taking effect.....

It is akin to the adage that world travel was out of the question when consensus had it that the world was flat....and we have paid a terrible price by our unwillingness to evolve: The loss of our manufacturing base, a weak recovery, and Trump as a candidate for president [i.e., his magical thinking /angry

constituency—i.e, with some overlap with Bernie]....it is a recipe for disaster!

Indeed, the over-flow crowds showing up at Bernie's rallies—and perhaps while not framed in the same words....is a protest against Washington for not making work a legal right—i.e., a protest against DC for clinging to the status quo, rather than evolving so that America will be in line with the 21st Century.

The bottom line is that UE is a NO ONE WINS: The jobless lose, civility loses [Ferguson, etc.], and the Market loses, to wit:

THE LAW OF DIMINISHED INCOME TO THE MARKET FROM UNEMPLOYMENT [hereafter D/UE LAW]

Short Definition:

> 3% is the zero-sum threshold above which unemployment starts substantially undermining the Market--and the loss in income to the Market is compounded exponentially with each percentage point of increase in unemployment, above 3%.

Ref: HR 1000 [in Committee]; FULL EMPLOYMENT IS A PRO-MARKET CONCEPT, and THE CASE FOR WORK BEING A LEGAL RIGHT, Amazon/Kindle

Jim Green, Democrat opponent to Lamar Smith, Congress, 2000

Thank you for contacting the White House!

CHAPTER TEN

President Obama/Council of Economic Advisers:

95% OF OUR SOCIAL ILLS WILL DISAPPEAR TOMORROW BY GETTING OUR FACTS AND PRIORITIES STRAIGHT....

We need look no further than Flint to readily see the devastation and injury to humans from unemployment [hereafter UE]—and documented in "Roger and Me". So why are we silent on the devastation to the Market, caused by UE? People do not buy what we manufacture when they are jobless....but whenever we talk about the evaporation of our manufacturing base....we blame outsourcing....rather than placing the blame where it most belongs—on our Job Creation incompetence! And fueled by the false and unworkable belief that "the market can provide anybody wanting a job, with a job." It is Pure BS...not supported by the data, and with a miserable record of Job Creation! And yet, it has been our sole Job Creation methodology since WW II....and via its incompetence, it has turned our inner-cities into war zones with an epidemic of gun violence....and a Rust Belt as Exhibit One!

The truth is: Unemployment is a NO ONE WINS....the jobless lose, civility loses [Ferguson, etc.,], and the Market loses, to wit:

THE LAW OF DIMINISHED INCOME TO THE MARKET FROM UNEMPLOYMENT [hereafter D/UE LAW]

Short Definition:

3% is the zero-sum threshold above which unemployment starts substantially undermining the Market--and the loss in income to the Market is compounded exponentially with each percentage point of increase in unemployment, above 3%.

Ref: HR 1000 [in Committee], THE CASE FOR WORK BEING A LEGAL RIGHT: Our Only Path To Prison Reform, and, FULL EMPLOYMENT IS A PRO-MARKET CONCEPT, Amazon/Kindle

Jim Green, Democrat opponent to Lamar Smith, Congress, 2000

CHAPTER ELEVEN

President Obama/Council of Economic advisers:

73% of Americans have expressed a generalized anger—but when pinned down they cannot give a specific reason.....mostly it is expressed as a feeling—and centers around the economy and jobs—and is most often stated as "We are moving in the wrong direction".....

The purpose of this letter is to brazenly offer an explanation—IMHO—and would bet the farm I have it on the nose....

For instance, both the Democrats and Republicans miss it by making "minimum wage" the issue in this election—rather than making "work", itself, the issue—and admittedly Republicans/Trump refer to the former dragging both feet—but this evening Trump grudgingly agreed on a $10 minimum wage, on O'Reilly—but no one is taking stock that a minimum wage is meaningless to a person who is jobless!

And as Trump rightly noted—the "official" jobless number of 8 million is a joke—i.e., with the DOL not counting persons who have given up—the true number is closer to 20 million unemployed Americans! And, we need look no further than Flint to understand the devastation caused by unemployment, and yet neither party is citing the CAUSE, in search of a solution!

That is, that we have a phony/baloney method of Job Creation in America—to use street language—and yet, Washington keeps perpetuating the lie that the market can provide all the jobs we need—it is PURE BS!

Further, the right to work and be productive member of society was a given in primitive societies, but lost in the Age of Industrialization—

It is a fact that a "do nothing" Republican Congress has Washington ground to a halt—to the detriment of America—but another factor, never discussed, is that a Washington that has been bought and paid for by Special Interests—is deaf, dumb and blind when it comes to finding a solution to our antiquated method of Job Creation!

But rather than admitting this—and sitting down at the table to find real solutions....Washington tries to paper over it, and/or pretend it doesn't exist....

We have the solution—we have the "legal authorization" on the books, to limit our UE to 3%--permanently—and pending legislation in Congress: HR 1000—So WHY is this not the NUMBER ONE issue in this election?

Ref: FULL EMPLOYMENT IS A PRO-MARKET CONCEPT, Amazon/Kindle

Jim Green, Democrat candidate for Congress, 2000

PS Apologize for CAPS—your software doesn't allow emphasis….

CHAPTER TWELVE

President Obama/Council of Economic Advisers:

THE HISTORY OF HUMPHREY-HAWKINS

The historic March On Washington, and Dr. King's "I had a dream" speech, in 1963, was a march for JOBS.

At that time, and to this day, our job creation in America has been based on the premise that "the market can provide anybody wanting a job, with a job—

And yet, only ONCE since WW II has this method of job creation resulted in an unemployment rate below 3%--in 1953—leaving millions jobless in its wake.

Following Dr. Kings death in 1968, civil rights leaders, including Jesse Jackson, annually marched on Dr. King's birthday for legislation that would address our pervasive unemployment in America.

Their demand was not without legal foundation. In 1946, President Truman signed into law the [FULL] EMPLOYMENT ACT OF 1946, to provide employment for our troops returning from WW II.

The 1%, however, balked at American employees having rights—particularly a right to employment [the model which exists to this day]—and the law was never implemented.

Ironically, Australia enacted a law similar to President Truman's Employment Act—and for the same reason—and for the next 30 years [and until the ill-winds of neo-liberalism in the mid-1970's] Australia's employment model was based on the premise that "anybody wanting to work should be able to find a job"—with 2% or less unemployment common. Australians still refer to this as their "Golden Age".

As a result of the demand by civil rights leaders for legislation, however, in 1978 President Carter signed into law—what is commonly known as the Humphrey-Hawkins Full Employment Act [15 USC § 3101].

The law provides the "legal authorization" for the creation of a "reservoir of public employees" anytime our unemployment in America exceeds "3%". That is, and to this day—at no time should our unemployment rate in America exceed 3%.

The money in politics, however, has prevented this law from being implemented!

Notwithstanding, a lone Congressman, Conyers [and a growing number of co-sponsors] has diligently worked to implement Humphrey-Hawkins [currently, deficit-neutral HR 1000, in Committee].

And, singularly, unemployment is the most pernicious problem facing America, today....

Ref: FULL EMPLOYMENT IS A PRO-MARKET CONCEPT, Amazon

Jim Green, Democrat opponent to Lamar Smith, 2000

Thank You!

Thank you for contacting the White House.

CHAPTER THIRTEEN

President Obama:

It is impossible to reform our broken criminal justice system—absent our creating a viable job creation program in America.

And while it is generally believed that we do have a job creation program, in fact, we do not!

We have the BELIEF that "the market can provide anybody wanting a job, with a job"—but the data shows that only ONCE since WW II has this belief resulted in an unemployment rate below 3%--in 1953— leaving millions jobless in its wake-- and has resulted in:

60% minority unemployment in our inner-cities, with drug economies, and an epidemic of homicides [i.e., not fixing unemployment has turned our inner-cities into war zones, and created a breeding ground for our inexplicable incarceration rate].

Further this "belief" has been a stumbling block in finding a solution for our pervasive unemployment--In short, we have not been looking for a solution—because our policy makers believe we have one—and apparently few have looked at the data….

Also, ignored in the discussion is that unemployment is a "social" problem, with adverse, and oft severe social consequences—both for the individual, as well as the larger society [i.e., it is the responsibility of the larger society to solve]—

With tentacles integral to all of the social problems facing Americans, today—for instance, ending unemployment is integral to Criminal Justice Reform, and the repair of our crumbling infrastructure....

Further, in 1975 we spent $5 educating our youth, for every $1 we spent on prisons.....by the mid-1990's [with the American people having been terrorized by the Willie Horton ad—and on an hysterical prison building spree] our competing tax dollars tipped in favor of prisons—and at present we spend more on prisons, than on educating our youth.

The irony in all of this is that we have the "legal authorization", on the books to reduce our unemployment rate to 3%, tomorrow [15 USC § 3101—and deficit-neutral HR 1000, currently in Committee]—and also ignored in this context, is that President Obama had a weapon in addressing our economic meltdown in 2008, not available to FDR—and that is the $800 billion in Social Security Insurance claims percolating up through our economy—and in the absence of which--We would be buried in another Great Depression!

Turning the page—and given "automation", alone, is critical going forward in the 21st Century—and is a "win-win"—the American people win, and the market wins....

Ref: FULL EMPLOYMENT IS A PRO-MARKET CONCEPT, Amazon

Jim Green, Democrat opponent to Lamar Smith, 2000

CHAPTER FOURTEEN

President Obama/Council of Economic Advisers:

Our network of market-driven economies [the OECD, including the U.S]—currently have a pernicious job creation modality—with resulting high and pervasive unemployment since the mid-1970's—and on a collision course with the future—i.e., given "automation", alone, fewer and fewer jobs are being created with each passing year, as we advance into the 21st Century....

This job creation modality is based on the erroneous propaganda/belief that "the market can provide anybody wanting a job, with a job"—and yet, only ONCE since WW II has this modality resulted in an unemployment rate below 3%--in 1953—leaving millions jobless in its wake, and has resulted in our inner-cities turning into war zones--with 60% minority unemployment, drug economies, and an epidemic of homicides.

The irony in this disaster, however, is that the U.S. correctly anticipated this result in 1978—and provided the American people with a solution, i.e., the "legal authorization" [15 USC § 3101] to limit our unemployment henceforth to "3%", and as we advance into the 21st Century—

With a ton of cash poured into our political system, and a mind-set with both feet planted on the plantation—-- special interests sabotaged this law to prevent its implementation—to the detriment of Americans, and America [ISIS is the least of our worries in America, when we have the Republican party]!

Unemployment is a "social" problem, with adverse social consequences….it is solely the province of the larger society to solve—and leaving the solution to anything as erratic as the market—as we do now—is patently absurd!

The bottom line is that unemployment is a NO ONE WINS….the jobless lose, civility loses, and the market loses, to wit:

THE LAW OF DIMINISHED INCOME TO THE MARKET FROM UNEMPLOYMENT [hereafter D/UE LAW]

3% is the zero-sum threshold above which unemployment triggers inflation by diminishing labor training and skills, under-utilizing capital resources, reducing the rate of productivity advance, increasing unit labor costs, reducing the general supply of goods and services--and the loss in income to the Market is compounded exponentially with each percentage point of increase in unemployment, above 3%.

Ref: HR 1000 [in Committee], and FULL EMPLOYMENT IS A PRO-MARKET SOLUTION, Amazon

Jim Green, Democrat opponent to Lamar Smith, 2000

Thank You!

Thank you for contacting the White House

CHPATER FIFTEEN

THE HISTORY OF HOW WE GOT WHERE WE ARE
[WW II to Present]

Following WW II, President Truman signed into law the [FULL] EMPLOYMENT ACT of 1946, to provide employment for our returning troops.

Ironically, half-way around the world, Australia codified into their law an almost identical Bill, and for the same reason—

Difference is—Australia actually put their law into effect, and over the next 30 years it was intrinsic to employment policy in Australia that "anybody wanting to work should be able to find a job"—and save for a brief recession in 1961/62 their unemployment was 2%, or less. This period is still referred to as their "Golden Age", in Australia.

Unforeseen by either country, however, in the mid-1970's the world economy underwent a major paradigm shift as a result of the colliding forces of automation, globalization, technology, etc., reaching a critical mass—in brief, an adjustment towards modernity—From a perverse perspective, we became victims of our success....

The instability caused by this transition, however, resulted in a malaise, and ushered in the ill-winds of greed-driven neo-liberalism with its indifference to unemployment, and the likes of Thatcher and Reagan—and the menace of this greed-driven agenda was exploded by Bush II, resulting in obscene disparities in wealth that persists, and is the cause of much friction between right and left, to this day.

It also ushered in high and pervasive unemployment throughout our market-driven economies, the OECD—with 6% unemployment in Australia now the norm, and double-digit unemployment common throughout the Eurozone, to this day.

As a result of the "malaise", however, the U.S. took an aggressive, pro-active role in addressing the, above, economic shift—and in 1978 President Carter signed into law one of the most important laws in the 20th Century--an expansion of President Truman's full employment, i.e., Pro-Market 15 USC § 3101--which provides a *"legal authorization"* to create a "reservoir of public employees" [*indispensable to the effective functioning of a 21st Century market economy*]--at any time our unemployment in America exceeds "3%"—

But in spite of 3% unemployment being the threshold point above which unemployment starts substantially undermining the Market—this *legal authorization* has never been implemented--

And in spite of deficit-neutral HR 1000, or The Neighbor-To-Neighbor Job Creation Act—A federally mandated Social Insurance, owned by our employed, to provide a fund to hire/train our unemployed—[more on the critical need to apply this job creation methodology in a 21st Century market economy, ahead]....

Ref: FULL EMPLOYMENT IS A PRO-MARKET CONCEPT, Amazon/Kindle

Jim Green, Democrat opponent to Lamar Smith, Congress, 2000

CHAPTER SIXTEEN

THE HISTORY OF HOW WE GOT WHERE WE ARE
[Mid-1970's to Present]

In the mid-1970's, the colliding forces of automation, technology, globalization, etc., reached a critical mass—resulting in a Market no longer capable of producing the jobs necessary to its viability, and causing ubiquitous unemployment in all of the OECD countries—and leaving their leaders conflicted, ever since, regarding the displaced employee. Eurozone unemployment is still in double digits, and Greece and Spain both in excess of 20%, plus. High unemployment was also a major factor in Arab Spring.

In the U.S., we took a pro-active role in addressing this economic shift—and in 1978 President Carter signed into law 15 USC § 3101--which "authorizes" the creation of a "reservoir of public employment" at any time our unemployment in America exceeds "3%".

In 1979, however, and in a panic over Humphrey-Hawkins—our ultra-conservative foundations, and desperate to promote the Supply-Side fraud, embraced a flawed paper by an obscure MIT student, David L. Birch "The Job Generation Process"; and [with lots of cash] gave his paper biblical importance, and every president since has cited his finding as gospel.

Birch's paper concluded that "small businesses" were the greatest generator of new jobs—problem is, for the purposes of policy-making—it is BS. In a study at Harvard University in 2010, "The Myth of Small Business Job Creation" The research shows "no systematic relationship between firm size and growth." And that small businesses can actually detract from job growth.

In spite of this, however, Washington struggles, still, to make this antiquated notion, work--that it is only the market that can create jobs—and the result has been a disaster, politically as well as otherwise!

It would be impossible to still have 7.8% unemployment—if we were on the right path—and among other problems with this concept--if the market fails, the unemployed are out of luck.

Further, unemployment is a "social" problem we are seeking to address with a highly unstable, incompatible entity: The Market

What apparently isn't clear going forward is that an expanding and contracting public workforce is an *indispensable* component to the *effective* functioning of a modern market economy—

The market thrives when we have a robust, employed, consuming workforce—and overlooked is that HR 1000 [currently in Committee], and the proposed "Neighbor-To-Neighbor Job Creation Act" www.Inclusivism.org [both authorized under Humphrey-Hawkins], are deficit-neutral--Pro-Market "win-win" solutions:

The American people win, and capitalism wins—

Jim Green, Democrat candidate for Congress, 2000

CHAPTER SEVENTEEN

Friends: In the event you have gotten this far—according to the Federal Election Commission, I am a candidate for president in the 2016 election—and rest assured I am not delusional, or like Trump…on an ego trip…..I filed solely to deliver a message—you are reading it—and to urge passage of the above legislation….

To Whom It May Concern—in Washingon:

OUR CHOICES ARE: Adapt and change in a world that is changing, whether we like it or not, OR be forced to create a Police State to hold our anachronistic policies, practices and laws in place—

And in America, today, we have chosen the latter…..and as only one pernicious example, of thousands—Ferguson is the result….

In a comedic, but religious context we hear of persons asking God for a sign—anything—which will warn us that we are on the wrong path, and need to change direction…..and our Police State choice, above, is *our sign*…..few are listening….

To illustrate a critical area in which we need to adapt and change in a 21st Century economy: We have far more work that needs to be done in America, than we have persons to fill these jobs—And 86% of Americans believe that "Anybody wanting to work should be able to find a job"---So, why on earth *in a democracy*, do we have 9 million jobless Americans—[per the 11/14 DOL Jobs report]?

The answer is because our *method* of job creation in America is based on a Fairy Tale! Specifically, our current *one and only* job creation methodology in America, is based on the myth/sacred cow:

"The market can provide anybody wanting a job, with a job"—

Problem is—it is pure BS—and only *once* since WW II has this methodology resulted in an unemployment rate below 3%--in 1953 [i.e., which translates into 5 million left jobless]--because the market *cannot* create enough jobs—in short, the jobs for this 5 million jobless--*don't exist*!

The right-wing propaganda mills trick our fools into believing that the market has created this 5 million jobs, but because those on welfare are "lazy and don't want to work" this 5 million jobs go unfilled—but that is *pure balderdash!*

The vast majority of persons on welfare, are there *because* the *market* cannot create enough jobs, i.e., the market lacks the viability to create these jobs—the jobs simply *do not exist*!

And as further proof, according to the CBO, on our current path it will be 2017 before America returns to even an anemic 5.5% unemployment rate [following the Great Recession] and if the market fails in the interim—the jobless are out of luck!

Further, this travesty is compounded because the Republicans cling to devious and discredited Supply Side Economics [to this day] as a solution, to wit:

Siphon America's wealth away from the consuming middle—give this windfall of cash to the Koch Bros [a metaphor for the 1%, hereafter "KB"]—they will build factories all across our fair land—everyone will have a job in the corporation—and we will all live happily ever after—Yes, folks it is a fairy tale!

And what we learned from this dark cloud over America is what Bush I called it long ago—before America was subjected to this devious scam—i.e., Supply-Side is "VooDoo Economics"!

So why have we allowed ourselves to be deceived by this Republican scam—[handcrafted by a plutocracy/oligarchy that still has one foot on the plantation]? But I don't want to giveaway the surprise ending—and some of my response isn't printable....! Further, and to say it up front....I am a capitalist—I support 100%: Build a better widget, sell it for a million bucks, and retire in South Florida....it is the Republican agenda, today, that is anti-market...more on this throughout.....

When President Carter handed the reigns over to Reagan in 1981—he left America with a very modest

$60 billion deficit—as a direct result of Supply-Side, however, when Republicans held the White House [Clinton actually cut the deficit]—this $60 billion ballooned to a staggering $10 trillion by 2008—and it has cost Americans an additional $7+trillion to clean up this Republican mess—

Ask any economist: Our only way out of a meltdown *is to buy our way out!* [it was the lesson learned from the Great Depression].

And anyone who thinks McCain, had he been elected, would not have addressed this with a Stimulus, the same as President Obama in 2009—is stuffed between the ears with rice pudding......

Further, we learned that we cannot siphon America's wealth away from the consuming middle, and give it to the "KB"—without sending our economy into meltdown—as occurred in 1987 and 2008—in short, the Supply-Side scam has a shelf-life of about 7 years before the economy collapses—and as noted, costing the taxpayers trillions to put a floor under a disappearing economy!

And another fallout/direct result from this dark chapter is the disparity in wealth it has created in America—AKA the "wealth gap"--and currently the "richest 1 percent in the United States now own more wealth than the bottom 90 percent"—the second highest in our history, the first was just before the Great Depression.

A couple of other factors that played into the above scenario—when every waking moment in capitalism is spent pondering how to eliminate as many of us humans, as possible, from the workplace—to increase "profits"—why, on Earth, would we look to the market to solve our unemployment crisis in America?

As well, few things on earth are more unstable than the market....we can count on one hand the number of corporations in America that were around in 1900....with tens of thousands long since disappeared; and given "automation", alone, the market will produce fewer and fewer jobs the further we advance into the 21st Century.

Further, unemployment is a "social" problem—we, as the larger society have the responsibility to solve—i.e., it is unrealistic to expect the market to solve this problem—the market is in the "for profit" business, not the social work business—and the former would not long be in business--if they were...for example, we should never condemn the CEO for closing a plant when they are losing money—but we should be outraged by a government that doesn't have a clue re the displaced employees.....

Also, unemployment is a *no one wins* .....the jobless lose, and market loses, to wit:

> 3% is the zero-sum threshold above which unemployment triggers inflation by diminishing labor training and skills, under-utilizing capital resources, reducing the rate of productivity

advance, increasing unit labor costs, and reducing the general supply of goods and services--and the loss in income to the Market is compounded exponentially with each percentage point of increase in unemployment, above 3%.

Short Definition:

3% is the zero-sum threshold above which unemployment starts substantially undermining the Market--and the loss in income to the Market is compounded exponentially with each percentage point of increase in unemployment, above 3%.

In sum, our job creation should be based on: Fix unemployment, and this will fix the market [HR 1000], rather than [our current mind-set] Fix the market, and this in turn fix unemployment [HR 2847] – with a result that has been a disaster—as we inch along in our job recovery, see data above, and when we didn't *Fix Unemployment* a retaliatory electorate ushered in a House filled with lunatics in the 2010 election, and then doubled down in 2014!

Look around—all signs in our economy are up—and yet over two-thirds of our rank and file believe "we are moving in the wrong direction"—their perception is that our economy is in the tank—that we are in an economic malaise—a condition that would disappear overnight if we did, in fact, *Fix Unemployment*!

Best guess is that Congress passed, and President Obama signed into law HR 2847 [the HIRE Act], in 2009—which is based on fix the market, and this will fix unemployment [180 degrees off course]—but they did this because of the pervasive [but false] *belief* that "The market can provide anybody wanting a job, with a job"—it is *pure BS......it doesn't work*! Had we insisted on putting a lawnmower engine in the rocket to get us to the Moon....we would never have gotten there...[same difference]....and all of the empirical evidence is proof HR 2847 didn't create anywhere near the jobs needed...

Jim Green, Democrat opponent to Lamar Smith, Congress, 2000

CHAPTER EIGHTEEN

HOPPER-READY: THE NEIGHBOR-TO-NEIGHBOR JOB CREATION ACT

[1] PROPOSED LEGISLATION:

THE NEIGHBOR-TO-NEIGHBOR JOB CREATION ACT

A Pro-Market, deficit-neutral, federally mandated, Social Insurance, owned by our employed, to provide a fund to hire/train our unemployed.

SECTION 1. SHORT TITLE.

This Act shall be cited as The Neighbor-To-Neighbor Job Creation Act [To establish employment/training opportunities for the unemployed in compliance with the "Legal Authorization" in Public Law 15 USC § 3101, for the creation of a "reservoir of public employees", anytime our unemployment rate exceeds "3%", with an emphasis on training for market needs, including a training stipend, where there is a shortage of trained workers--hereafter NTN].

SEC. 2. DEFINITIONS.

In this Act the following definitions apply:

    (1) SECRETARY- The term `Secretary' means the Secretary of Labor.

    (2) STATE- The term `State' has the meaning given such term in section 102(2) of the Housing and Community Development Act (42 U.S.C. 5302(2)).

    (3) TRUST FUND- The term `Trust Fund' refers to the Department of Labor Full Employment Trust Fund.

    (4) UNIT OF GENERAL LOCAL GOVERNMENT- The term `unit of general local government' has the meaning given such term in section 102(1) of the Housing and Community Development Act (42 U.S.C. 5302(1)).

    (5) URBAN COUNTY- The term `urban county' has the meaning given such term in section 102(6) of the Housing and Community Development Act (42 U.S.C. 5302(6)).

    (6) WEB SITE- The Secretary shall establish an Internet Web site to serve as an information clearinghouse for job training and employment opportunities funded by the Trust Fund.

SEC. 3. EMPLOYMENT OPPORTUNITY GRANTS TO STATES, LOCAL GOVERNMENT.

(a) Use of Funds-A recipient of a grant under this section shall use the grant primarily for infrastructure repair, including, but not limited to:

(A) The painting and repair of schools, community centers, and libraries.
(B) The restoration and revitalization of abandoned and vacant properties to alleviate blight in distressed and foreclosure-affected areas of a unit of general local government.
(C) The augmentation of staffing in Head Start, child care, and other early childhood education programs to promote school readiness and early literacy.
(D) The renovation and enhancement of maintenance of parks, playgrounds, and other public spaces.

Respectfully Submitted,

Jim Green, Democrat candidate for Congress, Dist 21, TX, 2000

CHAPTER NINETEEN

WHAT WE NEED TO DO GOING FORWARD IN THE 21ST CENTURY:

Inexplicably "public employment" is seen the same as WPA—where millions are employed directly by the federal government—when that model is not only outmoded—it is insufficient to address our problems in the 21st century.

What we need today is an expanding and contracting public workforce—that expands during downturns in the market, and contracts as employees return to the private sector [Google: The Buffer Stock Employment Model]—triggered anytime our unemployment exceeds "3%" [as "authorized" under Humphrey-Hawkins]-- and least understood: This is an INDISPENSABLE component in the effective functioning of our 21st Century Market.

The market thrives when we have a robust, employed, consuming workforce—our manufacturers are sitting on $2 trillion in cash because they do not have consumers for their products—i.e., absent consumers, they lay off employees—[and the Republican solution, Reaganomics, has acted as an accelerate to this downward spiral—and which Romney promises to return us to if he is elected]!

In short, the above model is a "win-win" solution—the American people win, and capitalism wins!

To achieve this, what is being urged is "The Neighbor-To-Neighbor Job Creation Act": A federally mandated, mutual insurance—owned by our employed [from janitor to CEO] to create a fund to hire/train our unemployed.

To be viable, however, our job creation solution _MUST_ contain:

1] Be based on the premise that we have far more work that needs to be done in America, than we have persons to fill these jobs.

2] It MUST have renewable funding.

3] It will not add a dime to our deficit.

To expand briefly, it is currently believed, erroneously, that we need "make work" jobs so that everyone who wants to work will have a job—but this is absurd—and an insult to "Yankee Ingenuity".

We do not have an unemployment crisis from a shortage of jobs, or money—but rather from a shortage of imagination.

Regarding "renewable funding" ALL of our job creation solutions, to date, have been based on the mind-set: "jump start" the market, and the market will in turn create all the jobs we need—

and even setting aside that this is untrue, our current job creation is moving at a snail's pace—long past the unemployment benefits drying up—with the CBO projecting that even with the JOBS Act, signed into law on April 6, 2012--it will be 2017 before we return to a barely acceptable 5.5% unemployment rate!

Further, by its nature when we "jump start" -- the employment ends when the funding runs out as we learned from the Stimulus—whereas any real fix to our unemployment crisis _demands_ renewable funding….

And whether the electorate will accept an unemployment rate hovering around 8% on election day—is the $64,000 question….

Regarding not adding a dime to our deficit— under The Neighbor-To-Neighbor Job Creation Act [NTN], the _funding_ to reduce our unemployment to 3% comes from an insurance owned by our employed, rather than added to our deficit—

If one is employed in America, participation in this insurance plan is mandatory—similar in concept to our auto insurance or Social Security

Insurance [and without question the most successful social program in American history].

Jobs beget jobs--And with a modest policy cost of 4% of salary we can create more "private-sector" jobs in 6 months, that HR 2847, and the JOBS Act, in 6 years—and unlike these laws—NTN will not add a dime to our deficit!

Finally, this is in total concert with the will of the American people, i.e., that "anybody willing to work should be able to find a job"—and the American people have told our politicians time and again of their willingness to chip in to help their neighbor get a job [and as an _insurance_, as above, it also protects their continued employment]—it is just that Washington is deaf as an adder!

CHAPTER TWENTY

President Obama/Council of Economic Advisers:

Public-Sector jobs strengthen our free-enterprise market economy—i.e., they are a critical component to the viability of our 21st Century economy--rather than weakening the market--as propagandist, with one foot on the plantation, fraudulently deceive the public into believing for the purposes of exploiting American employees.....

Indeed, since WW II, the Koch brothers [both literally, and a metaphor, here, for the 1%] have spent tens of millions buying governors and legislators, to cement "at will" employment in every state [and currently only Montana limits to probationary employees]; and to destroy "collective bargaining", i.e., unions in America—

In sum, they have spent tens of millions of dollars to destroy "employee rights" in America!

To understand the importance of "collective bargaining" for employees, it is informative to take a page from history:

When Hitler became the dictator in Germany, one of his first laws was to make it illegal for more than three persons to gather on the street—and German citizens were subject to immediate arrest if they did.

The same principal is being used by preventing employees putting their heads together, as it were, to bargain for employee rights—and recently one group of employees placed "job security" over a salary increase—with the irony being that the specific objective of "at will" employment—is to destroy "job security"!

In short, the deceptive propaganda to frighten Americans regarding "public-sector" jobs, has but a single parent: To exploit American labor—by some, to assuage deep-seated feelings of inferiority [they can only feel tall, by making others small, in their eyes]-—but most often for just pure GREED!

Where our policies makers go wrong by pandering to some in the oligarchy—and/or buying into this fraudulent propaganda:

Unemployment is a NO ONE WINS—the jobless lose, civility loses, and the market loses, to wit:

THE LAW OF DIMINISHED INCOME TO THE MARKET FROM UNEMPLOYMENT [hereafter D/UE LAW]

Short Definition:

> 3% is the zero-sum threshold above which unemployment starts substantially undermining the Market--and the loss in income to the Market is compounded exponentially with each

percentage point of increase in unemployment, above 3%.

Ref: IT IS IMPOSSIBLE TO BE A CHRISTIAN, AND VOTE REPUBLICAN, Amazon

Jim Green, Democrat opponent to Lamar Smith, 2000

CHAPTER TWENTY-ONE

JIM GREEN QUOTES:

- If we accepted that we are animals, perhaps we could then start acting more like human beings....

- Winners want others to win....

- HAPPINESS comes from within: It is something we owe to ourselves, not something another person can give or take away....

- We have far more work that needs to be done in America, than we have persons to fill these jobs....so why in the year 2017 do we "officially" have 8 million jobless Americans—and on credible evidence, 20 million?

- The plutocracy/oligarchy in America, still has one foot on the plantation....

- The right to work and be a productive member of society, was a given in primitive societies—but lost in the Age of Industrialization—to the detriment of civilization....

- When a person is without rights –criminal wrongdoing against that person is invisible....

- The greatest enemy of capitalism is not communism or socialism---it is unemployment.

- Unemployment is a "social" problem, we as the larger society have a fiduciary obligation to address....

- The unconscionable flaw is the belief that a legal right to work is an enemy of capitalism—the fear by the plutocracy/autocracy that Humphrey-Hawkins [the most vital legislation in the 20th Century] posed a threat to special interests, rather than an adjunct...
- Re us humans, we are not as far away from being savages as we like to think we are.....

CHAPTER TWENTY-TWO

I didn't write the following. It is a cut and paste from FACEBOOK, or some blog [would like to give credit if knew the author]--but it is so on target regarding how "fear" is driving Conservative policy in America today—i.e., is undermining America and our progress—and relegating America to a Third World country status, rather than a world leader—FDR had it on the nose in "All we have to fear, is fear itself"...at his inaugural in 1933....

"Conservatives are such cowards: they are afraid of gay people getting married or serving in the military; they are afraid of bringing terrorists to super max prisons in the US from which no one has ever escaped; they are afraid of the boy scouts letting gay kids in; they are afraid of everyone voting and are constantly suppressing the vote under some bogus voter fraud theory; they are afraid of letting students vote at their universities; they are afraid of women having the right to choose; they even are afraid of women getting contraception [the real issue actually is a women's agency and control over their bodies]; they are afraid of immigration reform leading to citizenship because they are afraid of-- name whatever reason; they are afraid of mandating gun purchasers to undergo background checks for crazy people and terrorists; they are afraid of people smoking pot; they are afraid of climate change being real and contradicting their beloved Bible; they are afraid of legitimate campaign reform; they are afraid of Muslims; they are afraid of blacks; they are afraid of atheists; they are afraid of hippies; they are afraid of socialists; they are probably still afraid of monsters under their beds; they are just rank cowards and keep making things up to be afraid of."

CHAPTER TWENTY-THREE

[I couldn't resist including this...and yes I am the author.....]

A MESSAGE FROM GOD

MANY CENTURIES AGO, a man of the cloth, we don't know his name, and in a flash of insight (perhaps induced by peyote) told his flock that "sex is a sin". And lo and behold he learned that by taking a very natural and healthy part of our life and turning it into something that was "dirty and nasty", that he could imprison his flock, and fill his coffers, and hallelujah it was a great day for the Lord!

Quickly, his miracle spread to other churches in his village, and then to the next village, and then the next county, and then state, and soon it spread to all the churches in the ancient world, and all of their flocks cowed in fear and shame and became imprisoned, and their coffers over-floweth. Hallelujah, it was a great day for the Lord!

And to keep the myth alive they started inventing stories, half-baked stories, that made no sense to anyone who is rational, such as "Mary was a virgin"— well, she just had to be a virgin because she would never partake in anything that was dirty and nasty, like sex (if you're doing it right), and this was necessary to make "sex is a sin" make sense...so they invented a Mary that was "sinless"--you get the picture. And their coffers over-floweth. Hallelujah, it was a great day for the Lord!

No one seemed to be bothered that when we play tricks on the human mind by taking something that is very natural and healthy, such as sex, and make it dirty and nasty that all kinds of bad things happen to the human mind:

Such as most pedophiles, and most serial killers, and voting Republican, and unwarranted suicides, and most mental illness, and unwanted pregnancies. (Teens not wanting to have sex is the perversion, not the other way around, and by replacing sex education and condoms, with unrealistic "abstinence", and by using blather about "low self-esteem" to shame them into not "sinning"—We have a teen pregnancy in the U.S. twice that of England and Canada!).

But none of this mattered, because their coffers over-floweth, and Hallelujah, it is a great day for the Lord!

There is a cure--------Tell our right-wing hypocrites, who Judge, rather than "Judge not".... to shove it....

GOD

ABOUT THE AUTHOR: I was employed in our Criminal Justice System for a cumulative 20 years as a probation officer, with 5 of those years as a chief probation officer. I authored the concept of "Shock Incarceration" which became law in Kansas in 1970, and then was adopted in numerous jurisdictions in the U.S. and also spread to Europe—it is currently identified in the U.S. as "Boot Camp" [as the means to "shock" the young offender—and a total distortion of my original intent—like many ideas, once released, they take on a life of their own]. I also instigated establishment of the first Court Psychiatric Clinic in the U.S., in conjunction with psychiatrists from the Menninger Foundation, as a chief probation officer. Finally, I was the Democrat candidate for Congress, District 21, TX, 2000. I would most define myself as a Social Ecologist-- [albeit my degree is in Psychology]. My web page is www.Inclusivism.org –which has been on the internet since 1996.
http://www.amazon.com/James-L.-Jim-Green/e/B001KHZIMM/ref=ntt_dp_epwbk_0

A BRIEF ADDENDUM: When the U.S. Supreme Court denied certiorari—where the violation of my constitutional rights were obvious, and criminal negligence on the part of the government defendants in the death of our son, equally obvious—[detailed in THE HARVARD BOYS CLUB, Amazon/Kindle]--I filed a Petition for Rehearing [which is automatic]—and included the following. The Clerk of the U.S. Supreme Court called me at my work in California, and asked that I withdraw the "cartoon" [a reprint from The NEW YORKER] from my Petition. I refused on the basis of the First Amendment, and it remains in the archives at the U.S. Supreme Court [Docket #: 79-1627], to this day. The wording [not that clear] is: "Excellent, excellent. A fine blend of truths, half-truths, and blatant falsehoods".

IN THE

Supreme Court of the United States

October Term, 1979

No. 79-1627

JAMES L. GREEN,

Petitioner,

VS.

"Excellent, excellent. A fine blend of truths, half-truths, and blatant falsehoods."

www.ingramcontent.com/pod-product-compliance
Lightning Source LLC
Chambersburg PA
CBHW071214220526
45468CB00002B/602